Conversations With The Father

God Is Speaking...Are You Listening?

By Joyce A. Thomas-Vinson

© 2016 by Joyce Thomas-Vinson

ALL RIGHTS RESERVED

Preface

Writing has always been a key part of who I am. In high school, I wrote for the yearbook and newspaper. As an adult, I have published newsletters in my church and on my job, and I write for and edit a magazine. Additionally, I teach English part time at a local community college.

For many years, I have kept a journal and written inspirations that have come to me through the Spirit. When I started keeping a journal, publishing was never a goal until a co-worker asked why I had not written a book. After my initial surprise, I realized that an element of my personal ministry is to encourage and inspire by sharing these messages.

This is not, nor is it intended to be, an in depth theological work. By sharing some of my conversations with God, I hope to encourage you to listen for the voice of God and remind you of some of his truths. I hope that something that I share inspires, encourages and reminds you that God is speaking.

Table of Contents

Chapter 1	Are You Listening?	5
Chapter 2	I Am Free	13
Chapter 3	Talking to Yourself	18
Chapter 4	Don't Let the Facts Fool You	24
Chapter 5	Prepare to Soar	27
Chapter 6	The Father Is Listening	32
Chapter 7	Wait On the Lord	36
Chapter 8	A Reason Behind This Season	40
Chapter 9	Re-position Your Weight	44
Chapter 10	In the Midst of the Storm	47
Chapter 11	What Do You Expect?	53
Chapter 12	After The Rain	58

CHAPTER ONE

Are You Listening?

*"He shall teach you all things, and bring all things to your remembrance." * **John 14:26**

I have wondered many times, and I have heard others ask, "How do I know when God is speaking to me?" I admit at times I have felt confused about what God was or was not saying to me, and some days I still strain to hear his voice. However, as I mature spiritually, I realize the Father speaks to his children at all times. The problem is we do not always listen. Let us first address some of the hindrances that prevent us from fully receiving messages from God.

One reason we miss his voice is because of what I call the *burning bush syndrome.* This refers to our tendency to wait for a dramatic presentation like God gave Moses when an angel of the Lord gave him an assignment from a burning bush in the midst of the dessert (Exodus 3), or a dire warning like the great fish that swallowed Jonah when he refused to go to warn the people of Nineveh about their wickedness (Jonah 1), or even a supernatural messenger like the donkey who spoke to Balaam in Numbers 22. If we are not careful, we can get so caught up looking for the sensational that we miss obvious messages in front of us. Admittedly, God does sometimes capture our attention in dramatic fashion. Frankly, we sometimes require extreme measures to make us take notice. However, he largely addresses us in more mundane ways. Think of our earthly parents. Although they sometimes shout or scream when they urgently need to get our attention, more often than not, they speak to us in conversational tones. Our heavenly Father, likewise, speaks to us in the common things and events around us.

We can be assured that God speaks to us because he is with us constantly. In Deuteronomy 31:6 we find, "*Be strong and of a good courage, fear not, nor be afraid of them: for the Lord thy God, he it is that doth go with thee; he will not fail thee, nor forsake thee"* (KJV). God promises never to leave us; indeed, he is with us at all times. In John 14:16 as Jesus prepares to leave his disciples, he reaffirms that the comforter will remain with them forever. *"And I will pray the Father, and he shall give you another Comforter, that he may abide with you for ever"* (KJV). Later in John 14: 25-26, Jesus confirms that God will speak to them and teach them through the Holy Spirit, *"These things I have spoken unto you, being yet present with you. But the Comforter, which is the Holy Spirit, whom the Father will send in my name, he shall teach you all things, and bring all things to your remembrance, whatsoever I have said unto you"* (KJV). So, God walks with us, talks with us, and instructs us at all times, and he does not need a grand stage or theatrics to get his message across. We need only learn to listen and allow the Holy Spirit to direct us.

Another reason we miss messages from God is because of *busyness.* Our lives can become so hectic that we do not make time to be still and listen to God. We live in a society that reinforces the notion that to be busy is a good thing. We rush to and from work (I myself admit to multiple jobs). We dash off to and from school, from school to play, to meetings, to church and back, and the endless *to do* list goes on. This constant motion creates a level of chaos and noise in our lives such that we do not have time to tend to our personal matters or hear ourselves think. When we become this distracted and overwrought, we most certainly are less inclined to listen for the voice of God. Now, I am not suggesting that we must sit still at all times. We have responsibilities and obligations. However, we must learn to prioritize and select those activities that really add value to our lives. Every hour does not have to be crammed beyond capacity.

I have been guilty of being in constant motion. Fortunately, I am learning that when I slow down and quiet my mind, body, and spirit, I become more aware of his constant presence, and I can hear God whisper to me in various ways. This is an activity I have grown to relish. One day on my way to work I drove leisurely along enjoying the quiet beauty of the morning. I came across a stand of trees on the side of the road adorned in their fall foliage. The colors were spectacular: bright yellow, orange and gold, deep red and burgundy, stubborn green and fading brown. As the October breeze blew, the leaves did a colorful dance against the brilliant blue back drop of the clear skies. I could only proclaim, "God is Awesome. Only the Master could create such a work of art."

Taking in that scene reminded me that God is ever present and in charge. I heard the Spirit of God admonishing me to calm down, slow down; quit striving and stressing, *"Be still, and know that I am God."* (Psalm 46:10, KJV). Had I been rushing as usual, I might have missed this beautiful, yet subtle reminder of who God is. I challenge you to slow down and listen; he is speaking.

Perhaps one of the most prevalent attributes that leads us to miss conversations with God is our need to prime the pump. The term priming the pump refers to using older pumps when a suction valve had to be primed with water in order to work properly. As an instructor at a local community college, I encourage my students to read over chapters before we discuss the material in class. This enables them to prime the pump by pouring some of the information into their consciousness in advance, so as I cover the subject matter in class they recognize the concepts and are prepared to take them in with greater clarity and understanding.

Sadly, this is the area where many Christians fall short. We do not sufficiently prime the pump. We do not take time to read and understand the word of God. The *truth* of his message does not change. As it is written in Matthew 24:35, *"Heaven and earth shall pass away, but my words shall not pass away"* (KJV). His word is consistent. Often when we say we need to hear from God, we are asking for some reinforcement or verification of his word. He gives us this daily, but if we are not versed in his word, we certainly cannot expect to recognize confirmation when he sends it.

We must read and study his word, and be prepared to receive him as he speaks to us. 2 Timothy 2:15 reinforces our necessity to study the word of God. *"Study to shew thyself approved unto God, a workman that needeth not to be ashamed, rightly dividing the word of truth"* (KJV). We cannot correctly interpret his word if we do not study it.

I am sure you have people in your life you recognize instantly when they call on the telephone. You recognize the sound of their voices, and you know the types of things they believe and would say. Even if they attempted to disguise their voices, you would still know them because you have spent time with them and have an established relationship.

John 1:1 tells us, *"In the beginning was the Word, and the Word was with God, and the Word was God"* (KJV). When we study the Word, which is God, we are spending time with and developing a relationship with him. John 10:27 reiterates this alliance: *"My sheep hear my voice, and I know them."* (KJV). Studying the word of God and getting to know him enables us to hear and discern his voice more clearly as he speaks to us daily. Likewise, as we speak to him in prayer, we get to know his voice and recognize his presence in our lives.

The fact is we all have periods when we feel that God is not speaking to us. In sharing some of my conversations with God, I hope to remind you of some of his truths and illustrate how he speaks to us. Since the God I serve is no respecter of persons, just as he speaks to me, he is speaking to you. I encourage you to get beyond the *burning bush syndrome*. God does not need dramatics to reach you. Reduce some of the *busyness* in your life, so you can find time to still your mind, body, and spirit long enough to hear from God. Then prime the pump by reading the Word. Get to know

God and develop a relationship with him, so when he is speaking you know it. His delivery may vary, but his truth is ever constant.

I pray my conversations with the Father will encourage and inspire you. Remember, the real question is not, "Is God to speaking to me?" Rather it is, "Am I listening?"

CHAPTER TWO

I Am Free

"Whom the son sets free, is free indeed." **John 8:36**

I am a great fan of the old sitcom *The Andy Griffith Show* which ran from 1960-1968. I love watching the episodes in syndication. The show depicts a small, simple town where everyone knows everybody else. The sheriff, Andy Taylor, played by Andy Griffith, is the central character who provides law and order without the use of a gun.

The characters are priceless. One of my favorites is Otis Campbell, the town drunk. Otis goes out and gets intoxicated every weekend then comes into the courthouse and locks himself in the jail cell. One day while laughing out loud as this scene played out, I heard the Spirit reminding me that many Christians do the same thing.

Many times we find ourselves bound by: strife, debt, drugs, lust, and more. But we do not have to remain captives. John 8:36 tells us, *"If the Son therefore shall make you free, ye shall be free indeed."* (KJV). Jesus has already set us free. When he went to the cross, he carried all of our sins and shortcomings with him to the grave. When he arose, he did so with the authority to overcome all of our imperfections. There was a price to be paid for sin, but Jesus paid that debt in full. When we accept Jesus as our Savior, we too are set free. We are free from sins past, present, and future. As joint heirs with Christ, we have the power to overcome everything on earth by evoking the name, the blood, and the power of Jesus.

We are no longer bound by sin or other situations in our lives. We only remain in bondage when we, like Otis, return to our captors. Many times we are satisfied to confess that certain issues in our lives are bad habits which we cannot break. We classify our actions as family traits that we are born with. We blame our circumstances. Leaning on this type of rationale allows us to escape responsibility for our choices and actions. We give in to our flesh, to lust, to confusion, to overspending and much more repeatedly as if we have no authority to break free. We continually return to these chains that bind us. We use any number of excuses to explain our behavior rather than acting and speaking like people with the God given authority to be more than conquerors.

In Acts 3, we read the story of the man at the gate of the temple which is called Beautiful who had been lame from birth. It was widely known that he was born with this affliction, so it was simply accepted as a part of him. But he encountered Peter and John after they had been baptized in the Holy Spirit. By faith, in an instant, he was set free from his indisposition. It did not matter that he had been thus afflicted since before he was born. Likewise, it does not matter how long you have dealt with issues and shortcomings. It does not matter if your struggle is with a family trait that has passed from one generation to the next. Nothing can hold you back in the presence of the Holy Spirit. Through Christ, you can be set free.

We also stay in bondage because of our focus. All too often, instead of keeping our hearts and minds on God and his word, we place our attention on our problems. We give the sin and shortcomings greater power when we concentrate on them rather than the deliverer.

In Acts 16, Paul and Silas are in prison in Philippi. At midnight, the darkest hour, they started praying and singing. They did not focus on the chains that literally bound them. They looked to and praised their God. As a result, there was an earthquake and the chains on their feet as well as the other prisoners were loosened. The liberator had come. In our darkest hour, we should emulate Paul and Silas. Psalm 22:3 tells us, *"But thou art holy, O thou that inhabitest the praises of Israel"* (KJV). Simply said, God inhabits the praises of his people, so he comes into our presence and into our situations when we praise him rather than our circumstances.

In Mark 5, we find the story of the man who was bound by the demons that possessed him. When Jesus asked the demon who he was, the demon told Jesus that he was Legion because they were many. Regardless of the large number of demons inhabiting the man, Jesus was still able to set him free in an instant. Thus, although you may be dealing with numerous issues that may appear overwhelming, Jesus can still free you from them all.

It is time to step away from the chains. Today, realize that as a child of God you are already free. You are not subject to the desires of the flesh that seek to keep you bound. Stop acting like Otis on Andy Griffith locking yourself in the cell. In 2 Corinthians 3:17 we find, *"Where the spirit of the Lord is, there is liberty"* (KJV). If the Holy Spirit resides within you, you are well and truly free. You have absolute power in the name of Jesus to overcome. Walk with the Lord, walk in your power, walk in your freedom, and throw away the keys. THEY have no power to keep you bound!!

CHAPTER THREE

Talking to Yourself

"For as he thinketh in his heart, so is he." **Proverbs 23:7**

Think of those you love dearly. Imagine watching them as they work their very best on a task, but fall short of perfection in completing the task. Would you walk up to them after they have given their best effort and tell them, "You are so stupid. You are such a failure. You never get anything right?" Would you watch them put on their Sunday best then tell them, "You're so fat and ugly?"

We do just this every day. We tell ourselves these things and much worse. I commonly hear people telling themselves disparaging things. For the majority of us, we would not dare say these hurtful things to a loved one. Unfortunately, we have no such qualms about making these remarks to ourselves. In fact, we confess negativity with such regularity that we no longer realize what we are doing. We must be mindful of the things we say when we are talking to ourselves.

Proverbs 23:7 tells us "*As a man thinketh in his heart, so is he*" (KJV). We cannot afford to think unfavorable things about ourselves because we manifest those things in our lives. Instead of thinking of ourselves in these terms, we need to bring our thoughts in line with what the word of God has to say about us. According to the word of God, his children are the *head, and not the tail; ... above not beneath... lenders not borrowers...blessed in the city and field (*Deuteronomy 28, KJV),...*able to do all things* (Philippians 4:13, KJV), ... *more than conquerors* (Romans 8:37, KJV),...*fearfully and wonderfully made* (Psalm 139:14, KJV).

In Matthew 12:34 we find, "*Out of the abundance of the heart the mouth speaketh*" (KJV). When we hold these positive, powerful words in our hearts, we start to confess them with our mouths. Subsequently, these thoughts and words start to manifest themselves in our lives.

Shortly after the birth of my children, who were born within two years of each other, I was feeling mentally and physically exhausted and drained. I loved my children and was grateful that God had entrusted them into my care, but they required an enormous amount of time and energy. I constantly felt tired, worn out, and helpless. I actually dreaded the days ahead of me. Deciding I wanted and deserved better, I started renewing my mind. I wrote some positive confessions about myself and placed them on the mirror, so I saw and spoke them every morning as I prepared for the day and every night before I went to bed. It did not happen overnight, but slowly my outlook shifted. I started feeling more positive, powerful, and confident. These affirmations infiltrated my thoughts, my words, my heart, even the way I carried and presented myself to the world. People started smiling at me, greeting me, and giving me positive feedback. The very things I confessed to myself daily were being manifested in my life, and people started speaking those things back to me.

One of the confessions was my favorite scripture, Philippians 4:13, "*I can do all things through Christ which strengtheneth me*" (KJV). I always ended my conversations with myself with this passage. Additionally, anytime I felt uncertain about a situation, I spoke these words aloud to myself. Over time, people started calling me to do printing projects, speak at their churches and schools, sing on programs, teach Sunday School and bible study, and even create costumes. It got to a point when I said, "These people act like they think I can do anything." I had confessed, "I can do all things" so long those words had manifested in my life. Thoughts and words do have power.

We have the ability to speak death or life into our situations. Proverbs 18:21 says, "*Death and life are in the power of the tongue*" (KJV). In the beginning, God stepped out on nothing and with his words created everything. Jesus used his words to call the dead back to life. In Luke 17:6, Jesus tells his disciples that we too have this power, "*And the Lord said, If ye had faith as a grain of mustard seed, ye might say unto this sycamine tree, Be thou plucked up by the root, and be thou planted in the sea; and it should obey you*" (KJV). We have the authority to speak the changes we want to see in our lives. If we keep our thoughts in line with the word of God, and we hide these words in our hearts, and our tongues follow suite, we start to walk in the will of God for our lives. Then we are no longer subject to the whims and circumstances surrounding us.

At one stage in my life, I was in a job where I was extremely unhappy. I had been dissatisfied in the position for several years, but I finally got to a point where I said, "Enough!" On Thursday, August 13, 1998, I prayed to God saying I knew he had something better for me, and I was proclaiming it. I reminded him of his word found in John 14:13-14: *"Whatsoever ye shall ask in my name, that will I do, that the Father may be glorified in the Son. If ye ask anything in my name, I will do it"* (KJV). I asked for a better job in Jesus' name. I even wrote the prayer down and included a calendar, so I could keep track of my request and God's response. On Sunday, August 16, 1998, I saw a job listing in the local newspaper that seemed perfectly suited to me. I told my nephew who was sitting near me, "This is my job right here."

On Monday, August 17, 1998, I faxed a cover letter and resume to apply for the job. On Tuesday, August 18, 1998, I received a call asking me to come in for an interview. I interviewed for the position Thursday, August 20, 1998, and

I had a follow up interview on Monday, August 24, 1998. On August 31, 1998, I was officially offered the job. I had spoken this change into my life, and I believed it until it came to pass.

Our thoughts and words have great power! We must remember to be careful what we say when we are talking to ourselves. Are your thoughts in line with the word of God? What are you saying to yourself when no one is listening? Are you confessing victory in life? You have the power. Think positively; speak positively; live positively!

CHAPTER FOUR

Don't Let the Facts Fool You

"Faith...the evidence of things not seen." **Hebrews 11:1**

I am such a football fanatic. I love to watch high school, college, and professional games. One day I was with my family watching my favorite college team play against one of its fiercest rivals, and it had gotten to the point that a loss for my team appeared to be a virtual certainty. My team had been undefeated to this point, but our hopes for a national championship were going down the drain.

It was the fourth quarter. The rivals were driving down the field with a few minutes remaining in the game. Throughout the afternoon, my team's defense had been incapable of stopping the opponent, especially on third down and long. To make matters worse, the offense had been anemic during the second half of the game. Several times in succession my team's possession of the ball had ended with no score. Without the ability to stop the opponents on defense or score any points on offense, the facts overwhelmingly indicated we were headed for the first defeat of the season. I already felt defeated.

I turned to my son (another staunch football fan) and asked, "What do you think?"

With no hesitation and without missing a beat, he responded with absolute certainty, "We're gonna win." He was absolutely resolute in his reply, and as he turned back to watch the last few minutes of the game play out, he showed no signs of distress, only a quiet assurance that all was well.

I, on the other hand, could not see how we could win. I was too caught up in what I could see. None of the facts seemed to support the conclusion that we would win. To my surprise, my team thwarted the opponent's final drive and held them to an unsuccessful field goal attempt. They then proceeded to drive the ball down the field and score a game winning touchdown with only seconds remaining on the clock.

Do not misunderstand me; I am NOT saying God had any team preference in the game. I am certain he has more important things to deal with. The lesson for me was my son's reaction. It was a great illustration of faith. When evidence says we are defeated, faith says we win! The Spirit reminded me of Hebrews 11:1 where we find, *"Faith is the substance of things hoped for, the evidence of things not seen"* (KJV). In other words, we are not limited to what we can see with our physical eyes or perceive with our minds. 2 Corinthians 5:7 says as Christians *"We walk by faith, not by sight"* (KJV). Plainly stated, it does not matter how circumstances and history appear. Our actions and outcomes are not restricted by what we see. All too often we block our blessings by confessing what we cannot see. Instead, we must trust God to do the impossible. We cannot allow the facts to fool us. We must walk in our victory even in the face of certain defeat. Regardless of the facts, WE WIN!

CHAPTER FIVE

Prepare to Soar

"They that wait on the Lord...shall mount up with wings as eagles." **Isaiah 40:31**

Recently while studying Isaiah 40:31, I came across a video of an eagle taking flight. It provided quite a revelation to this commonly quoted scripture. While watching the eagle prepare and take off, the Spirit brought to life many words from God.

The eagle was originally positioned on a stand, and before he actually left his perch, he did a little hop and raised his wings in an upward position. His hop reminded me that as we prepare to soar, we too must reposition ourselves. Romans 3:23 says, *"For all have sinned, and come short of the glory of God"* (KJV). Everyone has sinned by thought, word or deed. In reality we have done all three. 1 John 1:10 says, *"If* we say that we have not sinned, we make him a liar, and his word is not in us" (KJV). Thus, in order to soar we must first properly align ourselves. Because we have sinned, we must accept Jesus as our Lord and Savior and be reconciled with God. Once we are in a right relationship with God, we have access to all of his promises. We cannot realistically expect to continue doing things outside the will of God but still receive his blessings. We must get in position to receive what he has in store for us.

When the eagle raised his wings, I was struck by how massive they were in comparison to the size of his body. The wings are the power source which enables him to take flight. We too have a massive power source in our in lives. Philippians 4:19 says, *"But my God shall supply all your need according to his riches in glory by Christ Jesus"* (KJV). God is our omnipotent provider who supplies all of our needs. In the flesh, we are small and limited, but we are backed by a God who knows no limits, with whom nothing is impossible. *"For with God nothing shall be impossible"* (Luke 1:37, KJV). We have only to ask of him in the name of Jesus, and our petitions are met. We often come short of our needs because we do not fully realize the massive power that is ours in the Lord.

Then the eagle took off from his perch. He did not move slowly or hesitantly. He jumped from the perch and immediately began to flap his enormous wings vigorously. I imagine that he needed the velocity in order to actually take flight. This too provided a lesson. When we are on a mission for God we need to jump into the task with great intensity rather than stepping out hesitantly or slowly with doubt. We need to put our all into our work.

I love to start my mornings off with a hot cup of coffee, but there is nothing worse than taking a swig of tepid coffee. My general response is to immediately spit out the offending liquid. God has a similar response to our commitment. Revelations 3:16 tells us that we should be either hot or cold not lukewarm. Unfortunately, we often approach our Christian walk with lukewarm energy and dedication. Subsequently we do not "take flight" in the calling God has set before us. This lack of intensity results in many of us falling flat on our faces or remaining on the perch never taking flight, never soaring to the heights that God intended for us to achieve in our lives. If we hope to truly soar in our Christian walk, we must move with certainty and great vigor. We cannot afford to barely move or take half steps. We have to give it our all. It is time for us to take off!

Finally, when the eagle started to climb he looked upward with laser-like focus. He was looking on things above. Colossians 3:2 tells us that we should, "*Set our affections on things above*" (KJV). If we want to excel, to really soar, we have to look up: to our desired end, to the possible, to our power source which is God. Like the eagle, we must maintain our focus. Many of us cannot move higher because we are too busy looking down or back. We look at past mistakes and failures. We think on those who try to hold us down, but in so doing, we hinder our progress. I have an unfortunate habit of looking back while walking. I cannot tell you how many times I have walked into a wall or destroyed a display in the store because I was looking in the wrong direction. It is difficult, if not impossible, to move upward when you keep looking down or back.

Sometimes we fail to look up because we are so focused on the circumstances surrounding us that we get mired in these things and are unable to soar. We only see problems and limitations. If our minds are on negative things, we can easily lose focus of where we want to go, so we fall flat. As Christians, we should not focus on the negative. Philippians 4:8 says, "…*Whatsoever things are true, whatsoever things are honest, whatsoever things are just, whatsoever things are pure, whatsoever things are lovely, whatsoever things are of good report; if there be any virtue, and if there be any praise, think on these things*" (KJV). Instead, think on the good, and look up to God who is able to deliver us from all things.

Get in position to soar; take off with great intensity; look up to the master; look up to your desired end. God intends for you to soar.

The Father is Listening

"Whither shall I go from thy spirit?" **Psalm 139:7**

"Mommy." This single word can instantly gain my full attention. Most often my daughter addresses me in this manner. However, when the moniker is followed by the unspoken question mark it implies a need for a response, commonly in the form of assistance.

Several years ago, I was traveling with a group of students to work on a building project in Baldwin County, Alabama. This weeklong event was held over the university's spring break. Unfortunately, the system where my children attended school did not have the same break. I was leery of being away from my children for a full week. Before I left for the week, my daughter even had a nightmare that she needed me, but I was not there.

CHAPTER SIX

Conversations with the Father   32

The first night in Baldwin County, I learned that I would be sleeping in a room with thirty students. Sleep eluded me that night as I heard a symphony of songs, buzzes, pings, and pongs as e-mails, texts, and phone calls came throughout the night to the students inhabiting the room. In hopes of getting sleep on the second night, we agreed to put all cell phones on silent to avoid the myriad of notifications. I even went one step further and put in ear plugs to silence all intrusions on my sleep. True enough, silence fell in the room, and I drifted into a sound slumber.

At 4:30 a.m. I was instantly awakened by a text that simply said, "Mommy." Although my phone was on silent and my earplugs were firmly in place, the cry of my daughter resonated clearly in my spirit. She had awaken in the night feeling badly, and her instinct was to call me. I was instantly on the alert and told her what to take to help her feel better. I even stayed with her by phone until she felt better and went back to sleep.

The Spirit reminded me that God the Father is likewise on call for his children. Even more so than our earthly parents, God is ever present and knows what we are in need of before we even ask. *"For your Father knoweth what things ye have need of, before ye ask him"* (Matthew 6:8, KJV). All we have to do is call on him.

The best part is God is not limited by time and space. Our earthly parents can only be in one place at a time, but God is omnipresent. He is in all places at all times. There is no place that we can go and no experience we can endure that can prevent God from hearing our call. David refers to this in Psalm 139:7-10, *"Whither shall I go from thy spirit? or whither shall I flee from thy presence? If I ascend up into heaven, thou art there: if I make my bed in hell, behold, thou art there. If I take the wings of the morning, and dwell in the uttermost parts of the sea; Even there shall thy hand lead me, and thy right hand shall hold me"* (KJV).

In Romans 8:38-39 Paul confirms that neither time, space, nor creations of any kind can separate us from God, *"For I am persuaded, that neither death, nor life, nor angels, nor principalities, nor powers, nor things present, nor things to come, nor height, nor depth, nor any other creature, shall be able to separate us from the love of God"* (KJV).

At one point early in my career, I had a job that included housing as part of my compensation. I completed the job assignment that I had been hired to do. Subsequently, I was going to be without a pay check or a place to stay. I called on God in prayer, asking him for a job. As soon as I completed the prayer, my telephone rang. Yes, there was someone on the telephone offering me another job that happened to include housing in the compensation. God had answered my call so swiftly that it actually startled me! He had heard my cry and answered immediately.

There is a great assurance in knowing God is ever present. At all times in all places, our Father is listening. 1 John 5:15 tells us, *"And if we know that he hear us, whatsoever we ask, we know that we have the petitions that we desired of him."* All we have to do is call.

CHAPTER SEVEN

Wait On the Lord

"Wait I say on the Lord." Psalm 27:14

One evening while I was preparing for a bible study on waiting, the Spirit of God gave me a great illustration. He reminded me of riding the school bus as a child. I went to the bus stop each morning to catch the bus. I and the other kids in my neighborhood waited on the bus to pick us up. Occasionally, the bus came to the stop later than usual, and we started to get a little anxious, but inevitably the bus showed up.

The Spirit showed me how waiting on the Lord can be similar in nature. First, we went to the bus stop because of what we knew. We knew the bus route. Each year the schools distributed a schedule including the times and locations of the bus stops. Similarly, we wait on God because of what we know. We know who he is and what his promises are for all who will wait on him. As a child, I could not expect the bus to pick me up if I was in the wrong location. Likewise, we cannot expect to receive God's promises if we are not in the correct location according to his word. Occasionally, I was late getting to the bus station, but the bus driver had mercy on me and stopped to pick me up anyway. Does that sound familiar? How many times have we been in the wrong place at the wrong time spiritually or physically, but God, in his infinite mercy, picked us up anyway?

Next, as a child, I went to the bus stop because, based on prior experiences, I trusted the bus was coming to pick me up. I fully expected the bus to show up in time for school. After all, the route established the stops, and the bus had always come before. Because I knew the route, because the bus had always picked me up in the past, I expected the bus to stop every day. I believed the bus would run as planned. When I went to the bus stop the bus was not instantly there, but I had faith enough to stand still.

When we wait on the Lord, we must do so with faith and expectancy. In his word, God has given us his guidelines and his promises. Past experience has shown how God delivered his people from dire situations. In our own lives, we can see how God has picked us up. We have to believe he is going to do what he said. Sometimes in difficult situations, we may not necessarily see God moving on our behalf, but we have to have faith that he is going to do as he says. We must expect his promises to come to pass as long as we stay in his will and wait on him. We have to recall his words and remember what he has done for us in the past and faithfully hold on until he moves.

Occasionally, when we went to the bus stop, the bus arrived later than expected. We began to get anxious. We started looking down the road, wondering if it was coming around the corner soon. We started listening to the chatter that said it was not coming. We looked at our watches and wondered if we would be late for school. Even though it did not come precisely as expected, eventually, the bus showed up, and we were ultimately on time for school. I can still remember a few students who missed the bus completely because they gave up and left the bus stop. Some others were walking away when the bus rounded the corner. They had to run back to the stop to capture the bus.

In our Christian walk, we have similar situations. Sometimes we find ourselves waiting on God, but he does not come when we think he should. We start to get anxious. We start looking for other answers and solutions. Some of us lose faith and go elsewhere. Sometimes we doubt, but turn back to our faith in time to receive our blessings. Unfortunately, some lose faith altogether and miss out on the bridegroom like the five foolish virgins in Matthew 25:1-12. If we want to receive the promises of God, we must patiently wait. When the wait gets difficult and things start to look bleak we must remember who God is. We must recall how he has provided for us in the past. We must maintain our faith and hold on a little while longer. *"Wait, I say on the Lord"* (Psalm 27:14, KJV).

CHAPTER EIGHT

A Reason Behind This Season

"To every thing there is a season, and a time to every purpose under the heaven:" **Ecclesiastes 3:1**

I had a pastor whom I frequently heard say, "I am here for a season and for a reason." Although I heard him say this many times, in one particular instance the spirit of God really spoke to me regarding this statement. He reminded me we do experience various seasons in our lives, and they are, indeed, for a reason.

Just as the seasons transition from one to another, we have changes in our lives. This world is temporary and everything in it is, likewise, fading. In the third chapter of Ecclesiastes, Solomon gives an extensive list of things that we experience in our human form. We have periods of great joy such as the birth of a child, the completion of long sought after accomplishment, the marriage of a young couple, the appointment to a desired job. In these times, we dance, celebrate and give thanks.

Sometimes we experience seasons of victory and prosperity. If we are wise, we give God praise for his abundant blessings and guard against our human inclination to become proud or boastful. These periods give us an opportunity to acknowledge that all things come from God. Our successes provide the means for us to return a portion of our blessings to him and the building of his kingdom.

Other times we go through seasons of distress, the death of a loved one, the loss of a job, the disintegration of a treasured friendship. In these times, we can easily become disheartened or discouraged. We sometimes become angry and frustrated and question God. Because we see "darkly" and do not know in full, we cannot always readily see God preparing us through our seasons for even greater works, greater victory, and greater attainment. It is in our seasons of lack or distress that we must learn to trust God. We must be aware that he sees the full picture and knows what lies ahead for us. We must remember he makes no mistakes and is working things out for our good. Even when we do not fully comprehend the meaning and the reason for our season, we must be willing to walk by faith not by sight.

I have personally gone through some difficult seasons that seemed to go on endlessly. I cried out to God, "Where are you? Aren't you coming to deliver me?!" When I got on the other side of the trial, I realized as a result of what I had experienced and learned during my difficult times, I was prepared for and received even greater blessings on the other side.

In an earlier chapter, I recounted the story of waiting for a new job. While I waited, I gained additional skills through the assignments that I completed. I wrote articles for the newspaper and organized camps and conferences so that when the job came along looking for someone with that exact skill set, I was prepared.

Regardless of your season today, I encourage you to trust God and know that, "*All things work together for good to them that love God, to them who are the called according to his purpose*" (Romans 8:28, KJV). Because we have this assurance, we can declare like Paul in Philippians 4:11, *"I have learned, in whatsoever state I am, to be content"* (KJV). We can be assured whatever our season, God's grace is sufficient to see us through. So praise him in advance!!!

CHAPTER NINE

Re-position Your Weight

"Let us lay aside every weight." **Hebrews 12:1**

Years ago I had a wonderful dream that I could fly. I woke up feeling weightless, invigorated, and enlightened. It was such an intense feeling which made me want to share it with everyone who would listen. I still cannot find words adequate to fully describe the freedom and invigoration I felt.

In the dream, my husband and I are lifting weights in a gym. At one point I look over at my husband and discover he is flying. Understandably amazed, I ask my husband how he is able to fly. I want to do it as well. He responds, "You have to position your weight right." I follow his directions and reposition the weights, and sure enough I too am able to fly.

When I awoke from the dream, I felt so good I wanted to share the experience with everyone. Since that time, portions of the dream have returned on occasion, and I realize God is reminding me to position my weight correctly.

Can you identify some of the weights in your life? Have you ever been so burdened down by obligations that you literally felt heavy and sluggish? We all experience these feelings periodically. We are weighed down by caring for children and spouses. We are weighed down by financial concerns and obligations. We are weighed down by challenging jobs and relationships with co-workers. All of these things and many more keep us burdened down rather allowing us to fly.

But we can rise above it all. The word of God tells us, just as my husband told me in the dream, to position our weight correctly. As Hebrews 12:1 tells us, we must *"Lay aside every weight"* (KJV). We get bogged down trying to take care of everything by our might and power. This is contrary to the word of God. He knows we will have problems, but he tells us the way to handle those is to give them to him. 1 Peter 5:7 says, *"Casting all your care upon him; for he careth for you"*

(KJV). In other words, instead of trying to carry all of our burdens and concerns we need to place them in God's hand and allow him to take care of them. When we give our troubles to God, we are no longer bowed under the weight of those cares.

The word further tells us God knows what we need, but if we put him first he will take care of everything else. Luke 12:31 says, "*Seek ye first the kingdom of God, and all of these things shall be added unto you*" (KJV). In other words, all of our other earthly concerns should be placed behind seeking God. When we correctly put him first, all of our other needs are met.

We need to reposition our personal weights. Rather than being overcome with anxiety and worrying about the cares of our lives, we should seek him first, give all other cares to God, and allow him to handle the rest. When we learn to truly position our weights correctly, we can fly.

CHAPTER TEN

In the Midst of the Storm

"And he arose, and rebuked the wind, and said unto the sea, Peace, be still. And the wind ceased, and there was a great calm." **Mark 4:39**

Have you ever been in a storm? Growing up in the south, I have experienced tornados and hurricanes. I have felt the winds blow so hard that I thought I would be tossed away. I remember Hurricane Eloise which hit the area in September of 1975 when I was in elementary school. The storm was heading our direction, so we were being released from school. A neighbor came to pick me up, and as we went to the car, a gust of wind came through so strongly that my neighbor had to lift me from the ground to prevent me from being toppled over. This memory is all the more powerful, because I can see spiritually how God lifts me into his arms when the storms of life threaten to sweep me away. God is our shelter protecting us in times of storm.

I remember Hurricane Opal, which came through in the October 1995. The powerful storm ripped massive pecan trees from their roots and laid them down as if they were weightless. It was absolutely astonishing to pass by and see an orchard of pecan trees lying on the ground. My family faced this on an intimate level. In my mother's yard were two huge, long standing pecan trees. A neighbor who had passed by the house, called my mom to make certain she was okay because in his words, "I saw the devastation."

To my family's surprise, at some point during the hurricane, both huge trees were uprooted and literally draped over the house, the yard, and the street. God had been such a shelter that until the phone call, they were not even aware that the massive trees had fallen. God was their refuge. No harm came upon them in the midst of the storm.

In more recent times during an early spring weekend, the weather forecasts called for thunderstorms and the possibility of tornados. My son and I were out running errands, when I noticed the skies darkening. Dark, angry clouds raced across the sky. The winds picked up velocity, and the tree limbs swayed in the breeze. I knew a storm was imminent. I told my son, "It looks like the bottom is about to fall out. We need to hurry and get in the house." After arriving at home, and getting settled in, I noticed that the threatening storm had dissipated. In the midst of the storm, God had calmed the winds.

In another instance, I was sleeping soundly through the night. In the middle of the night, there was a shift in the atmosphere that woke me instantly. I sat up straight in the bed, listening and waiting. I am not certain whether it was the same atmospheric shift or my movements, but shortly thereafter, my husband awoke as well. It was storming! The rain was pounding on the rooftop. The winds were howling through the trees. It was a serious storm. I felt something was out there.

My husband and I got out of bed and starting looking out the windows. Shortly thereafter, we heard the distant cry of the sirens, indicating a tornado had been spotted. My husband asked if we should get the children out of bed and into a safe place. I felt an over whelming urge to walk around the house and pray, so we did. For a few more minutes the winds continued howling, the rain kept pouring, and the thunder and lightning persisted in putting on a show. We continued to walk around and pray. Then in an instant, I felt a shift in the atmosphere. I knew the danger had passed. I told my husband, "We can go back to bed now." As we settled back into the bed, the winds died down. The rain changed from threatening to a comforting white noise, and we were able to go back to sleep. In the midst of the storm, God had once again been our refuge and calmed the winds and the rain.

Of course, we know all of our storms are not physical. We have all types of storms in our lives. Sometimes, we feel as if life is battering us on every side. We have financial troubles pounding on the rooftops disturbing our sleep. We have family heartache and disappointment howling through our personal landscapes threatening to uproot our very existence. We have trouble on our jobs that threaten to overwhelm us. We have sickness and death that come like a thief threatening to rip our lives apart. If we are honest, we sometimes find ourselves being battered by multiple issues at one time. We cry out, "God, don't you see I'm in trouble. Don't you care? When are you going to come see about me?"

In Mark 4:37-40, Jesus and his disciples were on a ship when a great storm arose and caused the disciples to become fearful. To make matters worse, while the storm was raging, Jesus was asleep. When the disciples woke Jesus, he spoke simply, "*Peace, be still*" (Mark 4:39, KJV). Instantly, in the midst of the storm, the winds stopped. The water receded. There was great calm.

In the midst of our storms, it is imperative that we remember regardless of our situation, he can call peace into our storms. As Jesus quieted the storm, he says to his disciples, "*Why are ye so fearful? How is it that ye have no faith*" (Mark 4:40, KJV)? Even though the disciples had walked with Jesus daily and seen his miracles, in the face of the storm they were still fearful and lacking in faith. We are just like the disciples. As his children, we have seen him perform wonders in our lives, but when we encounter trouble, we start to fret and worry and cry out, "God, where are you!"

We must learn to trust as Hebrews 13:8 says, *"Jesus Christ is the same yesterday and today and forever"* (KJV). Just as he has brought us through situations in the past, he can do the same today, tomorrow, and forever. We must have enough faith to trust him. We have to know even in the midst of our storms we have peace; he is our refuge, and he can calm the winds.

CHAPTER ELEVEN

What Do You Expect?

"Let down your nets for a draught." **Luke 5:4**

One day while scanning the internet, I came across a quote from Mary Webb that said, *"The well of Providence is deep. It's the buckets we bring to it that are small."* After seeing this statement, the Spirit of God immediately reminded me of the passage of scripture in Luke 5:4-6.

In this passage, we see Simon who has spent a fruitless night fishing. He is approached by Jesus who enters the boat and in essence uses it as a pulpit from which to speak to the crowd gathered to hear his word. After speaking to the people, Jesus tells Simon to *"Launch out into the deep, and let down your nets for a draught"* (Luke 5:4, KJV).

Simon responds in verse 5 by saying, *"Master, we have toiled all the night, and have taken nothing: nevertheless at thy word I will let down the net*" (KJV). His response illustrated his low expectations. Simon's words indicated he was fully aware that he had toiled all night and come up empty. The statement Simon makes clearly implies that after a tiring, fruitless night, he does not expect anything different this time.

Have you faced situations where you have expended great time and energy on long, strenuous labor that bears no results? We all feel this way sometimes. Often, even in the presence of the Master we, like Simon, see our challenges first although the answer to whatever we need is within our immediate grasp. As a result of our futile efforts, we start to presume the worst possible outcomes. We start to expect minimal results rather than great success. Because we expect to fail, we do not prepare for victory. We set ourselves up for failure. In Simon's case, because he had worked through the night without catching any fish, he was not prepared for his large haul. In our own lives, we often confess defeat before we begin the task at hand, thereby setting the stage for failure.

Not only did his words indicate low expectations, but Simon's actions demonstrated the same. Jesus told Simon to let down his nets, but in his words Simon says he lowered his net. He obeyed the master partially. Does that sound familiar? Rather than letting down nets, Simon let down his net which was insufficient to hold his harvest, and it subsequently broke. True, he did end up with two boats full of fish, but imagine how much greater his blessing could have been if he had not suffered from low expectations. What if he had thrown out every net he could find? Could he have had multiple nets filled with fish? Fortunately, Jesus blessed Simon in spite of his doubt.

Many of us are like Simon. We suffer from low expectations. We enter into situations looking to fail rather than preparing to succeed. We do not expect to get the job, so we do not go into the interview fully committed and it comes across in our demeanor and responses to questions, so we miss out on the job. We go to the doctor assuming we will hear bad news, and we get it. We expect poor service when we go into businesses. After all, this company always gives poor customer service. So we go into the company ready for a fight and we get one.

There is a fast food restaurant that my sister and I frequently visit. In her experiences, she always has trouble.

If I ask her to stop by the establishment, her response is that they never get anything right. I can practically guarantee when she goes there she comes back angry because her presumption of poor service has proven true. I, on the other hand, frequent the restaurant often. I anticipate they are going to be prompt and courteous, and the vast majority of the time, that is the type of service I get. My food, accompanied by a smile, is delivered quickly. In most cases we get what we expect.

So what about you? Do you expect the best? Do you expect to prosper? Do you expect to get that job? Do you expect to own that business? Do you expect to fill the pews of your church with people on fire for God? Do you expect to love your neighbor and have them love you in return? It is time to expand our outlook. Our expectations are seeds that we are sowing. Subsequently, we reap those things that we plant through expectancy. 1 Corinthians 2:9 tells us, "*Eye hath not seen, nor ear heard, neither have entered into the heart of man, the things which God hath prepared for them that love him*" (KJV). There is a vast world of opportunity before us that we have not yet even began to imagine. It is time to raise our expectations. In the words of the Master, lower your nets. It is time for a huge harvest.

CHAPTER TWELVE

After the Rain

"W*eeping may endure for a night, but joy cometh in the morning.***" Psalm 30:5**

During an early spring storm, the rain pounded relentlessly. It did not appear that it would ever stop. There were floods and forecasts of even more flooding. At one point, I looked out the window at the water cascading downhill through the yard. The force of the rushing water picked up debris as it swept along its path. Leaves, pine cones, pine straw, and small twigs accompanied it as it rushed through the yard, down the road, into the storm drains.

As night fell, the storm continued. Throughout the night, I heard the steady pounding of the rain. I imagined the soggy, muddy mess that would remain after the rains. Near the breaking of day, the rain stopped and quiet returned.

When I looked out the window that morning, I was amazed by what I saw. The sun shone brightly. The sky was an undisturbed expanse of pale blue. The trees were filled with a fresh new crop of green leaves. The yellow pollen that had previously covered every available surface had been washed away. Everything appeared new. After all of the rain, it was a truly magnificent day.

Throughout the morning as I completed my household chores, I continued to marvel over the stunning beauty of the day. There was barely any evidence of the torrential rains that had fallen for two days. During this time of reflection, the Spirit of God reminded me that this event is similar to our human experiences.

In Matthew 5:45, we find the words, "*For he maketh his sun to rise on the evil and on the good, and sendeth rain on the just and on the unjust*" (KJV). In other words, we all have some rain in our lives. We have financial storms. We face illness, disease, and death. We wrestle with numerous difficulties and challenges. No one is immune to troubles. It indeed rains on the just as well as the unjust. But as Christians we have the assurance found in Psalm 30:5, "*Weeping may endure for a night, but joy cometh in the morning"* (KJV). Regardless of how relentless our storms may be, God can bring joy in the morning.

In Genesis chapters 6-8, we see the story of how God used the rain to sweep away the violent and evil men from the face of the earth. After making certain that Noah and his family and the animals to replenish the earth were safely enclosed in the ark, God used the water to destroy everything remaining on the earth. Yet after the rain, the inhabitants of the ark were able to come forth and create a new generation of mankind. There was new life after the rain.

When we realize that some rains come to sweep away the debris that clutter our lives, we can more readily see the sunshine after the rain. Just as the rain washed away the pollen and the debris from my yard, the challenges that we endure can wash away garbage from our lives. Have you ever lost an alleged friend who abandoned you during your storm? Truly you were better off without them in your life after the rain. I know some people who have faced health scares that forced bad habits and poor diets out of their lives. They too are all the better for having been purged of habits that robbed them of a quality of life. They are undoubtedly restored and better after the rain.

As I continued to reflect, the Spirit of God brought to my remembrance the last few months of my mother's life. Her illness throughout the summer was a torrential rain in our personal lives. We endured surgery, therapy, intensive care, heart failure and eventually death. It was a downpour! During one lull in the rain, my mother was much improved. She and I were together in her hospital room. She was eating, talking and very much alert. I was convinced that the storm was almost over. I mentioned an event that would take place in the near future, but she quickly told me she would be dead by then. I told her not to say that since she was obviously so much better. She responded by reiterating that she would not be around much longer. She assured me that she did not mind dying, but there were some other things that bothered her because in her words, "I haven't always been so good."

I realized she was concerned about her eternal life because she felt she would have to pay for past sin. This was my opportunity to reassure her. I told her, "You don't go to heaven because you've been so good. You go to heaven because you realize that you haven't been good, but you accept that Jesus died for your sin."

She looked at me as if she was pondering what I said. Then she asked, "Is that so?"

I answered, "Yes, you don't have to be perfect to go to heaven or no one would make it to heaven. We all sin and fall short. That's why Jesus died for us."

She seemed satisfied with that answer, and we went on to discuss other topics. I learned that she later told my sister that she was ready to go, and when my sister asked her where she was going, "Heaven," was her definitive answer.

My mother had come to peace with the fact that Jesus saves. During the rain that was her illness, this clutter and baggage that remained in my mother's spirit were washed away. She experienced fully what it meant to be new in Christ.

A couple months after this incident, my mother died. The night she transitioned, I went home, and to my total surprise I slept soundly through the night. No, I was not happy to lose my mom, but I realized after the rain there was peace. I could rest because I no longer had to sleep on edge wondering if she was okay. After the rain, the doubt, worry, and anxiety that hovered like menacing clouds over my days had been washed away. Now, I had peace. I knew there was no more pain, no more sickness, and no more medical emergencies. Now, I knew she was safe in the bosom of the Master, the one who loved and cared for her better than we ever could. 2 Corinthians 5:8 tells us, *"To be absent from the body, and to be present with the Lord."* The rains had cleared away and been replaced with new life and peace that surpasses human understanding.

When you face those inevitable trials, be encouraged. There is peace, restoration, and newness of life after the rain.

Your Turn

Now, it is your turn. Did any of these stories call forth personal memories? Can you recall times when God spoke to you in your daily walk? Can you see how God has worked through circumstances and situations in your life? I would love to hear your stories.

Email me at Joycetv@yahoo.com

Check out my blog at:

https://duchessthomas.wordpress.com/

Made in the USA
Monee, IL
07 March 2021

62141315R00038